# Irish Folk Stories for Children

## T. CROFTON CROKER

ILLUSTRATED BY

### FRANCES BOLAND

I am sure you both
will have lots of
enjoyment from this one
and Patrick might
enjoy it as well.
The guy that wrote this
book Croked it.
Best wishes from
Tony + Dottie

THE MERCIER

**The Mercier Press Limited**
4 Bridge Street, Cork
24 Lower Abbey Street, Dublin 1

This selection © The Mercier Press, 1983

Reprinted 1986
This Edition 1991

ISBN 0 85342 919 7

These stories were first published in *Fairy Legends and Traditions of the South West of Ireland* in 1825.

Printed in Ireland by Colour Books Ltd., Dublin.

# Contents

# 1

## Legend of Bottle-Hill

'Come, listen to a tale of times of old,
 Come, listen to me —.'

It was in the good days when the little people, most impudently called fairies, were more frequently seen than they are in these un-believing times, that a farmer, named Mick Purcell, rented a few acres of barren ground in the neighbourhood of the once celebrated pre-ceptory of Mourne, situated about three miles from Mallow and thirteen from the beautiful city called Cork. Mick had a wife and family. They all did what they could, and that was but little, for the poor man had no child grown up big enough to help him in his work; and all the poor woman could do was to mind the children, and to milk the one cow, and to boil the potatoes, and carry the eggs to market to Mallow. But with all they could do, 'twas hard enough on them to pay the rent. Well, they did manage it for a good while, but at last came a bad year, and the little grain of oats was all spoiled, and the chickens died of the pip, and the pig got the measles — she was sold in Mallow and brought almost nothing, and poor Mick found that he hadn't enough to half pay his rent.

'Why, then, Molly,' says he, 'what'll we do?'

'Wisha, then, what would you do but take the cow to the fair of Cork and sell her?' says she, 'and Monday is fair day, and so you must go tomorrow, that the poor beast may be rested for the fair.'

'And what'll we do when she's gone?' says Mick, sorrowfully.

'I don't know, Mick; but sure God won't leave us without, Mick; and you know how good he was to us when poor little Billy was sick, and we had nothing at all for him to take — that good doctor gentleman at Ballydahin came riding and asked for a drink of milk, and how he gave us two shillings, and how he sent the things and bottles for the child, and gave me my breakfast when I went over to ask a question, so he did, and how he came to see Billy, and never left off his goodness till he was quite well?'

'Oh! you are always that way, Molly, and I believe you are right after all, so I won't be sorry for selling the cow, but I'll go tomorrow, and you must put a needle and thread through my coat, for you know 'tis ripp'd under the arm.'

Molly told him he should have everything right, and about twelve o'clock next day he left her, getting a charge not to sell his cow except for the highest penny. Mick promised to mind it, and went his way along the road. He drove his cow slowly through the little stream which crosses it and runs under the old walls of Mourne. As he passed he glanced his eye upon the towers and one of the old elder trees, which were only then little bits of switches.

'Oh, then, if I only had half the money that's buried in you, 'tisn't driving this poor cow I'd be now! Why, then, isn't it too bad that it should be there covered over with earth, and many a one besides me wanting? Well, if it's God's will, I'll have some money myself coming back.'

So saying he moved on after his beast. 'Twas a fine day, and the sun shone brightly on the walls of the old abbey as he passed under them. He then crossed an extensive mountain tract, and after six long miles he came to the top of that hill — Bottle-Hill 'tis called now, but that was not the name of it then, and just there a man overtook him. 'Good morrow,' says he.

'Good morrow, kindly,' says Mick, looking at the stranger, who was a little man, you'd almost call him a dwarf, only he wasn't quite so little neither. He had a bit of an old, wrinkled, yellow face, for all the world like a dried cauliflower, only he had a sharp little nose, and red eyes, and white hair, and his lips were not red, but all his face was one colour, and his eyes never were quiet, but looking at everything, and although they were red they made Mick feel quite cold when he looked at them. In truth he did not much like the little man's company, and he couldn't see one bit of his legs nor his body, for though the day was warm, he was all wrapped up in a big great coat. Mick drove his cow something faster, but the little man kept up with him. Mick didn't know how he walked, for he was almost afraid to look at him, and to cross himself, for fear the old man would be angry. Yet he thought his fellow-traveller did not seem to walk like other men, nor to put one foot before the other, but to glide over the rough road — and rough enough it was — like a shadow, without noise and without effort. Mick's heart trembled within him, and he said a prayer to himself, wishing he hadn't come out that day, or that he was on Fair Hill, or that he hadn't the cow to mind, that he might run away from the bad thing — when, in the midst of his fears, he was again addressed by his companion.

'Where are you going with the cow, honest man?'

'To the fair of Cork then,' says Mick, trembling at the shrill and piercing tones of the voice.

'Are you going to sell her?' said the stranger.

'Why, then, what else am I going for but to sell her?'

'Will you sell her to me?'

Mick started — he was afraid to have anything to do with the little man, and he was more afraid to say no.

'What'll you give for her?' at last says he.

'I'll tell you what, I'll give you this bottle,' said the little one, pulling a bottle from under his coat.

Mick looked at him and the bottle, and, in spite of his terror, he could not help bursting into a fit of laughter.

'Laugh if you will,' said the little man, 'but I tell you this bottle is better for you than all the money you will get for a cow in Cork — ay, than ten thousand times as much.'

Mick laughed again. 'Why then,' says he, 'do you think I am such a fool as to give my good cow for a bottle — and an empty one, too. Indeed, then, I won't.'

'You had better give me the cow, and take the bottle — you'll not be sorry for it.'

'Why, then, and what would Molly say? I'd never hear the end of it, and how would I pay the rent? And what would we all do without a penny of money?'

'I tell you this bottle is better to you than money; take it, and give me the cow. I ask you for the last time, Mick Purcell.'

Mick started. 'How does he know my name?' he wondered.

The stranger proceeded, 'Mick Purcell, I know you, and I have a regard for you; therefore do as I warn you, or you may be sorry for it. How do you know but your cow will die before you go to Cork?'

Mick was going to say 'God forbid!' but the little man went on (and he was too attentive to say anything to stop him; for Mick was a very civil man, and he knew better than to interrupt a gentleman, and that's what many people, that hold their heads higher, don't mind now).

'And how do you know but there will be much cattle at the fair, and you will get a bad price, or maybe you might be robbed when you are coming home? But what need have I to talk more to you, when you are determined to throw away your luck, Mick Purcell.'

'Oh! no, I would not throw away my luck, sir,' said Mick, 'and if I was sure the bottle was as good as you say, though I never liked an empty bottle, although I had drunk the contents of it, I'd give you the cow in the name — —'

'Never mind names,' said the stranger, 'but give me the cow. I would not tell you a lie. Here, take the bottle, and when you go home do what I direct exactly.'

Mick hesitated.

'Well, then goodbye, I can stay no longer. Once more, take it and be rich; refuse it and beg for your life, and see your children in poverty, and your wife dying for want — that will happen to you, Mick Purcell!' said the little man with a malicious grin, which made him look ten times more ugly than ever.

'Maybe 'tis true,' said Mick, still hesitating. He did not know what to do — he could hardly help believing the old man, and at length in a fit of desperation, he seized the bottle. 'Take the cow,' said he, 'and if you are telling a lie, the curse of the poor will be on you.'

'I care neither for your curses nor your blessings, but I have spoken truth, Mick Purcell, and that you will find tonight, if you do what I tell you.'

'And what's that?' says Mick.

'When you go home, never mind if your wife is angry, but be quiet yourself, and make her sweep the room clean, set the table out right, and spread a clean cloth over it, then put the bottle on the ground, saying these words: "Bottle, do your duty", and you will see the end of it.'

'And is that all?' says Mick.

'No more,' said the stranger. 'Goodbye, Mick Purcell — you are a rich man.'

'God grant it!' said Mick, as the old man moved after the cow, and Mick retraced the road towards his cabin, but he could not help turning back his head, to look after the purchaser of his cow, who was nowhere to be seen.

'Lord between us and harm!' said Mick. 'He

can't belong to this earth, but where is the cow?' She too was gone, and Mick went homeward muttering prayers, and holding fast to the bottle.

'And what would I do if it broke?' thought he. 'Oh! but I'll take care of that,' so he put it into his bosom, and went on anxious to prove his bottle, and doubting of the reception he should meet from his wife. Balancing his anxieties with his expectations, his fears with his hopes, he reached home in the evening, and surprised his wife, sitting over the turf fire in the big chimney.

'Oh! Mick, are you come back? Sure you did not go all the way to Cork? What has happened to you? Where is the cow? Did you sell her? How much money did you get for her? What news have you? Tell us everything about it.'

'Why then, Molly, if you'll give me time, I'll tell you all about it. If you want to know where the cow is, 'tisn't Mick can tell you, for the never a know does he know where she is now.'

'Oh! then, you sold her, and where's the money?'

'Arrah! stop awhile, Molly, and I'll tell you all about it.'

'But what is that bottle under your waistcoat?' said Molly, spying its neck sticking out.

'Why, then, be easy now, can't you,' says Mick, 'till I tell it to you,' and putting the bottle on the table, 'That's all I got for the cow.'

His poor wife was thunderstruck. 'All you got! And what good is that, Mick? Oh! I never thought you were such a fool, and what'll we do for the rent, and what ——'

'Now, Molly,' says Mick, 'can't you listen to reason? Didn't I tell you how the old man, or whatsoever he was, met me — no, he did not meet me neither, but he was there with me — on the big hill, and how he made me sell him the cow, and told me the bottle was the only thing for me?'

'Yes, indeed, the only thing for you, you fool!' said Molly, seizing the bottle to hurl it at her poor husband's head; but Mick caught it, and quietly (for he minded the old man's advice) loosened his wife's grasp, and placed the bottle again in his bosom. Poor Molly sat down crying, while Mick told her his story, with many a crossing and blessing between him and harm. His wife could not help believing him. particularly as she had as much faith in fairies as she had in the priest, who indeed never discouraged her belief in the fairies; maybe he didn't know she believed in them, and maybe he believed in them himself. She got up, however, without saying one word, and began to sweep the earthen floor with a bunch of heath; then she tidied up everything, and put out the long table, and spread the clean cloth, for she had only one, upon it, and Mick, placing the bottle on the ground, looked at it and said, 'Bottle, do your duty.'

'Look there! Look there, mammy!' said his chubby eldest son, a boy about five years old — 'Look there! Look there!' and he sprang to his mothers's side, as two tiny little fellows rose like light from the bottle, and in an instant covered the table with dishes and plates of gold and silver, full of the finest victuals that ever were seen, and when all was done went into the bottle again. Mick and his wife looked at everything with astonishment, they had never seen such plates and dishes before, and didn't think they could ever admire them enough, the very sight almost took away their appetites. But at length Molly said, 'Come and sit down, Mick, and try and eat a bit, sure you ought to be hungry after such a good day's work.'

'Why, then, the man told no lie about the bottle.'

Mick sat down, having put the children to the table, and they made a hearty meal, though they couldn't taste half the dishes.

'Now,' says Molly, 'I wonder will those two good little gentlemen carry away these fine things again?' They waited, but no one came, so Molly put up the dishes and plates very carefully, saying, 'Why, then, Mick, that was no lie sure enough but you'll be a rich man yet, Mick Purcell.'

Mick and his wife and children went to their beds, not to sleep, but to settle about selling the fine things they did not want, and to take more land. Mick went to Cork and sold his plate, and bought a horse and cart, and began to show that he was making money, and they did all they could to keep the bottle a secret. But for all that, their landlord found it out, for he came to Mick one day and asked him where he got all his money — sure it was not by the farm, and he bothered him so much, that at last Mick told him of the bottle . His landlord offered him a deal of money for it, but Mick would not give it, till at last he offered to give him all his farm for ever. So Mick, who was very rich, thought he'd never want any more money, and gave him the bottle. But Mick was mistaken — he and his family spent money as if there was no end of it, and to make the story short, they became poorer and poorer, till at last they had nothing left but one cow, and Mick once more drove his cow before him to sell her at Cork fair, hoping to meet the old man and get another bottle. It was hardly daybreak when he left home, and he walked on at a good pace till he reached the big hill. The mists were sleeping in the valleys and curling like smoke wreaths upon the brown heath around him. The sun rose on his left, and just at his feet a lark sprang from its grassy couch and poured forth its joyous matin song, ascending into the clear blue sky,

> Till its form like a speck in the airiness blending,
> And thrilling with music, was melting in light.

Mick crossed himself, listening as he advanced to the sweet song of the lark, but thinking, notwithstanding, all the time of the little old man, when, just as he reached the summit of the hill, and cast his eyes over the extensive prospect before and around him, he was startled and rejoiced by the same well-known voice, 'Well, Mick Purcell, I told you you would be a rich man.'

'Indeed, then, sure enough I was, that's no lie

for you, sir. Good morning to you, but it is not rich I am now — but have you another bottle, for I want it now as much as I did long ago, so if you have it, sir, here is the cow for it.'

'And here is the bottle,' said the old man, smiling, 'you know what to do with it.'

'Oh! then, sure I do, as good right I have.'

'Well, farewell for ever, Mick Purcell, I told you you would be a rich man.'

'And goodbye to you, sir,' said Mick, as he turned back; 'and good luck to you, and good luck to the big hill — it wants a name — Bottle-Hill — Goodbye, sir, goodbye.' So Mick walked back as fast as he could, never looking after the white-faced little gentleman and the cow, so anxious was he to bring home the bottle. Well, he arrived with it safely enough, and called out as soon as he saw Molly — 'Oh! sure I've another bottle!'

'Arrah! then, have you? Why, then, you're a lucky man, Mick Purcell, that's what you are.'

In an instant she put everything right, and Mick, looking at his bottle, exultingly cried out, 'Bottle, do your duty.' In a twinkling, two great stout men with big cudgels issued from the bottle (I do not know how they got room in it), and belaboured poor Mick and his wife and all his family till they lay on the floor, when in they went again. Mick, as soon as he recovered, got up and looked about him. He thought and thought, and at last he took up his wife and his children and, leaving them to recover as well as they could, he took the bottle under his coat and went to his landlord, who had a great company. He got a servant to tell him he wanted to speak to him, and at last he came out to Mick.

'Well, what do you want now?'

'Nothing, sir, only I have another bottle.'

'Oh! oh! is it as good as the first?'

'Yes, sir, and better. If you like I will show it to you before all the ladies and gentlemen.'

'Come along, then,' So saying, Mick was brought into the great hall, where he saw his old bottle standing high up on a shelf, 'Ah! ha!' says he to himself, 'maybe I will have you by and by.'

'Now,' says his landlord, 'show us your bottle.' Mick set it on the floor, and uttered the words. In a moment the landlord was tumbled on the floor; ladies and gentlemen, servants and all, were running, and roaring, and sprawling, and kicking, and shrieking. Wine cups and salvers were knocked about in every direction, until the landlord called out, 'Stop those two devils, Mick Purcell, or I'll have you hanged.'

'They'll never shall stop,' said Mick, 'till I get my own bottle that I see up there on top of that shelf.'

'Give it down to him, give it down to him, before we are all killed!' says the landlord.

Mick put his bottle in his bosom, in jumped the two men into the new bottle, and he carried them home. I need not lengthen my story by telling how he got richer than ever, how his son married his landlord's only daughter, how he and his wife died when they were very old, and how some of the servants, fighting at their wake, broke the bottles. But still the hill has the name upon it, ay, and so 'twill be always Bottle-Hill to the end of the world, and so it ought, for it is a strange story!

# 2

# The Giant's Stairs

On the road between Passage and Cork there is
an old mansion called Ronayne's Court. It may
be easily known from the stack of chimneys and
the gable ends, which are to be seen, look at it
which way you will. Here it was that Maurice
Ronayne and his wife Margaret Gould kept
house, as may be learned to this day from the
great old chimney-piece, on which is carved
their arms. They were a mighty worthy couple,
and had but one son, who was called Philip,
after no less a person than the King of Spain.

Immediately on his smelling the cold air of
this world the child sneezed, which was naturally taken to be a good sign of his having a clear
head, and the subsequent rapidity of his learn-
ing was truly amazing, for on the very first day
a primer was put into his hand, he tore out the
A, B, C page, and destroyed it, as a thing quite
beneath his notice. No wonder then that both
father and mother were proud of their heir,

who gave such indisputable proofs of genius, or, as they call it in that part of the world, *genus*.

One morning, however, Master Phil, who was then just seven years old, was missing, and no one could tell what had become of him. Servants were sent in all directions to seek him, on horseback and on foot, but they returned without any tidings of the boy, whose disappearance altogether was most unaccountable. A large reward was offered, but it produced no news, and the years rolled away without Mr and Mrs Ronayne having obtained any satisfactory account of the fate of their lost child.

There lived, at this time, near Carrigaline, one Robert Kelly, a blacksmith by trade. He was what is termed a handy man, and his abilities were held in much esteem by the lads and the lasses of the neighbourhood; for, independent of shoeing horses, which he did to great perfection, and making plough-irons, he interpreted dreams for the young women, sang Arthur O'Bradley at their weddings, and was so goodnatured a fellow at a christening that he was gossip to half the country round.

Now it happened that Robin had a dream himself, and young Philip Ronayne appeared to him in it at the dead hour of the night. Robin thought he saw the boy mounted upon a beautiful white horse, and that he told him how he was made a page to the giant Mahon Mac Mahon, who had carried him off, and who held his court in the hard heart of the rock. 'The seven years — my time of service — are clean out, Robin,' said he, 'and if you release me this night I will be the making of you for ever after.'

'And how will I know,' said Robin — cunning enough, even in his sleep — 'but this is all a dream?'

'Take that,' said the boy, 'for a token' — and at the word the white horse struck out with one of his hind legs, and gave poor Robin such a kick in the forehead, that thinking he was a dead man, he roared as loud as he could after his brains, and woke up calling a thousand murders. He found himself in bed, but he had the mark of the blow, the regular print of a horse-shoe upon his forehead as red as blood; and Robin Kelly, who never before found himself puzzled at the dream of any other person, did not know what to think of his own.

Robin was well acquainted with the Giant's Stairs, as, indeed, who is not that knows the harbour? They consist of great masses of rock, which, piled one above another, rise like a flight of steps, from very deep water, against the bold cliff of Carrigmahon. Nor are they badly suited for stairs to those who have legs of sufficient length to stride over a moderate-sized house, or to enable them to clear the space of a mile in a hop, step and jump. Both these feats the giant Mac Mahon was said to have performed in the days of Finnian glory; and the common tradition of the country placed his dwelling within the cliff up whose side the stairs led.

Such was the impression which the dream made on Robin that he determined to put its truth to the test. It occurred to him, however, before setting out on this adventure, that a plough-iron may be no bad companion as, from experience, he knew it was an excellent knock-down argument, having, on more occasions than one, settled a little disagreement very quietly. So, putting one on his shoulder, off he marched, in the cool of the evening, through Glaun a Thowk (the Hawk's Glen) to Monkstown. Here an old gossip of his (Tom Clancey by name) lived who, on hearing Robin's dream, promised him the use of his skiff, and moreover offered to assist in rowing it to the Giant's Stairs.

After a supper which was of the best, they embarked. It was a beautiful still night, and the little boat glided swiftly along. The regular dip of the oars, the distant song of the sailor, and sometimes the voice of a belated traveller at the ferry of Carrigaloe, alone broke the quietness of the land and sea and sky. The tide was in their favour, and in a few minutes Robin and his gossip rested on their oars under the dark shadow of the Giant's Stairs. Robin looked anxiously for the entrance to the Giant's palace which, it was said, may be found by any one seeking it at midnight, but no such entrance could he see. His impatience had hurried him there before that time, and having waited a considerable space in a state of suspense not to be described, Robin, with pure vexation, could not help exclaiming to his companion, "'Tis a pair of fools we are, Tom Clancey, for coming here at all on the strength of a dream.'

'And whose doing is it,' said Tom, 'but your own?'

At the moment he spoke they perceived a faint glimmering of light to proceed from the cliff, which gradually increased until a porch big enough for a king's palace unfolded itself almost on a level with the water. They pulled the skiff directly towards the opening, and Robin Kelly, seizing his plough-iron, boldly entered with a strong hand and a stout heart. Wild and strange was that entrance, the whole of which appeared formed of grim and grotesque faces, blending so strangely each with the other that it was impossible to define any; the chin of one formed the nose of another; what appeared to be a fixed and stern eye, if dwelt upon, changed to a gaping mouth; and the lines of the lofty forehead grew into a majestic and flowing beard. The more Robin allowed himself to contemplate the forms around him, the more terrifying they became, and the stony expression of this crowd of faces assumed a savage ferocity as his imagination converted feature after feature into a different shape and character. Losing the twilight in which these indefinite forms were visible, he advanced through a dark and devious passage, whilst a deep and rumbling noise sounded as if the rock was about to close upon him and swallow him up alive for ever. Now, indeed, poor Robin felt afraid.

'Robin, Robin,' said he, 'if you were a fool for coming here, what in the name of fortune are you now?' But, as before, he had scarcely

spoken, when he saw a small light twinkling through the darkness of the distance, like a star in the midnight sky. To retreat was out of the question, for so many turnings and windings were in the passage that he considered he had but little chance of making his way back. He therefore proceeded towards the bit of light, and came at last into a spacious chamber, from the roof of which hung the solitary lamp that had guided him. Emerging from such profound gloom, the single lamp afforded Robin abundant light to discover several gigantic figures seated round a massive stone table as if in serious deliberation, but no word disturbed the breathless silence which prevailed. At the head of this table sat Mahon Mac Mahon himself, whose majestic beard had taken root, and in the course of ages grown into the stone slab. He was the first who perceived Robin and instantly starting up, drew his long beard out from the huge piece of rock in such haste and with so sudden a jerk that it was shattered into a thousand pieces.

'What seek you?' he demanded in a voice of thunder.

'I come,' answered Robin, with as much boldness as he could put on, for his heart was almost fainting within him — 'I come,' said he, 'to claim Philip Ronayne, whose time of service is out this night.'

'And who sent you here?' said the giant.

''Twas of my own accord I came,' said Robin.

'Then you must single him out from among my pages,' said the giant, 'and if you fix on the wrong one, your life is the forfeit. Follow me.' He led Robin into a hall of vast extent, and filled with lights, along either side of which were rows of beautiful children all apparently seven years old, and none beyond that age, dressed in green, and every one dressed exactly alike.

'Here,' said Mahon, 'you are free to take Philip Ronayne, if you will, but, remember, I give but one choice.'

Robin was sadly perplexed; for there were hundreds upon hundreds of children; and he had no very clear recollection of the boy he sought. But he walked along the hall by the side of Mahon as if nothing was the matter, although his great iron dress clanked fearfully at every step, sounding louder than Robin's own sledge battering on his anvil.

They had nearly reached the end without

speaking, when Robin seeing that the only means he had was to make friends with the giant, determined to try what effect a few soft words might have.

''Tis a fine wholesome appearance the poor children carry,' remarked Robin, 'although they have been here so long shut out from the fresh air and the blessed light of heaven. 'Tis tenderly your honour must have reared them!'

'Ay,' said the giant, 'that is true for you, so give me your hand, for you are, I believe, a very honest fellow for a blacksmith.'

Robin at the first look did not much like the huge size of the hand, and therefore presented his plough-iron, which the giant seizing, twisted in his grasp round and round again as if it had been a potato stalk and on seeing this all the children set up a shout of laughter. In the midst of their mirth Robin thought he heard his name called and, all ear and eye, he put his hand on the boy who he fancied had spoken, crying out at the same time, 'Let me live or die for it, but this is young Phil Ronayne.'

'It is Philip Ronayne — happy Philip Ronayne,' said his young companions, and in an instant the hall became dark. Crashing noises were heard, and all was in strange confusion, but Robin held fast to his prize, and found himself lying in the grey dawn of the morning at the head of the Giant's Stairs with the boy clasped in his arms.

Robin had plenty of gossips to spread the story of his wonderful adventure — Passage, Monkstown, Carrigaline — the whole barony of Kerricurrihy rung with it.

'Are you quite sure, Robin, it is young Phil Ronayne you have brought back with you?' was the regular question, for although the boy had been seven years away, his appearance now was just the same as on the day he was missed. He had neither grown taller nor older in look, and he spoke of things which had happened before he was carried off as one awakened from sleep, or as if they had occurred yesterday.

'Am I sure? Well, that's a queer question,' was Robin's reply, 'seeing the boy has the blue eyes of the mother, with the foxy hair of the father; to say nothing of the wart on the right side of his little nose.'

However Robin Kelly may have been questioned, the worthy couple of Ronayne's Court did not doubt that he was the deliverer of their child from the power of the giant Mac Mahon, and the reward they bestowed on him equalled their gratitude.

Philip Ronayne lived to be an old man; and he was remarkable to the day of his death for his skill in working brass and iron, which it was believed he had learned during his seven years' apprenticeship to the giant Mahon Mac Mahon.

# 3

# The Soul Cages

Jack Dogherty lived on the coast of the County Clare. Jack was a fisherman, as his father and grandfather before him had been. Like them, too, he lived all alone (but for the wife), and just in the same spot. People used to wonder why the Dogherty family were so fond of that wild situation so far away from all human kind, and in the midst of huge shattered rocks, with nothing but the wide ocean to look upon. But they had their own good reasons for it.

The place was just the only spot on that part of the coast where anybody could live well. There was a neat little creek where a boat might lie as snug as a puffin in her nest, and out from this creek a ledge of sunken rocks ran into the sea. Now when the Atlantic, according to custom, was raging with a storm and a good westerly wind was blowing strong on the coast, many a richly laden ship went to pieces on these rocks; and then the fine bales of cotton and tobacco, and such like things, and the pipes of wine, and the puncheons of rum, and the casks of brandy, and the kegs of Hollands that used to come ashore! Dunbeg Bay was just like a little estate to the Dohertys.

Not but they were kind and humane to a distressed sailor, if ever one had the good luck to get to land; and many a time indeed did Jack put out in his little currach which would breast the billows like any gannet to lend a hand towards bringing off the crew from a wreck. But when the ship had gone to pieces and the crew were all lost, who would blame Jack for picking up all he could find?

'And who is the worse of it?' said he. 'For as to the king, God bless him, everybody knows he's rich enough already without getting what's floating in the sea.'

Jack, though such a hermit, was a good-natured, jolly fellow. No other, sure, could ever have coaxed Biddy Mahony to quit her father's snug and warm house in the middle of the town of Ennis and to go so many miles off to live among the rocks, with the seals and sea-gulls for next door neighbours. But Biddy knew that Jack was the man for a woman who wished to be comfortable and happy; for, to say nothing of the fish, Jack had the supplying of half the gentlemen's houses of the country with the Godsends that came into the bay. And she was right in her choice, for no woman ate, drank or slept better, or made a prouder appearance at chapel on Sundays than Mrs Dogherty.

Many a strange sight, it may well be supposed, did Jack see, and many a strange sound did he hear, but nothing daunted him. So far was he from being afraid of Merrows, or such beings, that the very first wish of his heart was to fairly meet with one. Jack had heard that they were mighty like Christians, and that luck had always come out of an acquaintance with them. Never, therefore, did he dimly discern the Merrows moving along the face of the waters in their robes of mist but he made direct for them; and many a scolding did Biddy, in her own quiet way, bestow upon Jack for spending his whole day out at sea and bringing home no fish. Little did poor Biddy know the fish Jack was after!

It was rather annoying to Jack that, though living in a place where the Merrows were as plentiful as lobsters, he never could get a good view of one. What vexed him more was that both his father and grandfather had often seen them, and he even remembered hearing, when a child, how his grandfather, who was the first of the family that had settled down at the creek, had been so intimate with a Merrow that only for fear of vexing the priest he would have had him stand for one of his children. This, however, Jack did not well know how to believe.

Fortune at length began to think that it was only right that Jack should know as much as his father and grandfather did. Accordingly, one day when he had strolled a little farther than usual along the coast to the north, just as he turned a point he saw something like nothing he had ever seen before perched upon a rock at a little distance out to sea. It looked green in the body, as well as he could discern at that distance, and he would have sworn, only the thing was impossible, that it had a cocked hat in its hand. Jack stood for a good half-hour straining his eyes and wondering at it, and all the time the thing did not stir hand or foot. At last Jack's patience was quite worn out, and he gave a loud whistle and a shout, when the Merrow (for such it was) started up, put the cocked hat on its head and dived down, head foremost, from the rock.

Jack's curiosity was now excited and he

constantly directed his steps towards the point. But still he could never get a glimpse of the sea-gentleman with the cocked hat, and with thinking and thinking about the matter, he began at last to think he had only been dreaming. One very rough day, however, when the sea was running mountains high, Jack Dogherty determined to have a look at the Merrow's rock (for he had always chosen a fine day before), and then he saw the strange thing cutting capers upon the top of the rock, and then diving down, and then coming up, and then diving down again.

Jack had now only to choose his time (that is, a good blowing day), and he might see the man of the sea as often as he pleased. All this, however, did not satisfy him — he wished now to get acquainted with the Merrow, and even in this he succeeded. One tremendous blustering day before he got to the point from where he had a view of the Merrow's rock, the storm came on so furiously that Jack was obliged to take shelter in one of the caves which are so numerous along the coast, and there to his astonishment he saw sitting before him a thing with green hair, long green teeth, a red nose and pig's eyes. It had a fish's tail, legs with scales on

them, and short arms like fins; it wore no clothes, but had the cocked hat under its arm, and seemed engaged thinking very seriously about something.

Jack with all his courage was a little daunted, but thought it's now or never and so up he went boldly to the cogitating fishman, took off his hat and made his best bow.

'Your servant, sir,' said Jack.

'Your servant, kindly, Jack Dogherty,' answered the Merrow.

'To be sure, then, how well your honour knows my name!' said Jack.

'Is it I not know you name, Jack Dogherty? Why, man, I knew your grandfather long before he was married to Judy Regan your grandmother! Ah, Jack, Jack, I was fond of that grandfather of yours; he was a mighty worthy man in his time. I never met his match above or below, before or since, for sucking in a shellful of brandy. I hope, my boy,' said the old fellow, with a merry twinkle in his little eyes, 'I hope you're his own grandson!'

'Never fear me for that,' said Jack. 'If my mother had only reared me on brandy, 'tis myself that would be a sucking infant to this hour!'

'Well, I like to hear you talk so manly. You

and I must be better acquainted, if it were only for your grandfather's sake. But, Jack, that father of yours was not the thing — he had no head at all.'

'I'm sure,' said Jack, 'since your honour lives down under the water, you must be obliged to drink a power to keep any heat in you in such a cruel, cold, damp place. Well, I've often heard of Christians drinking like fishes, and might I be so bold to ask where you get the spirits?'

'Where do you get them yourself, Jack?' said the Merrow, twitching his red nose between his forefinger and thumb.

'Hubbubboo,' cries Jack, 'now I see how it is. But I suppose, sir, your honour has got a fine dry cellar below to keep them in.'

'Let me alone for the cellar,' said the Merrow, with a knowing wink of his left eye.

'I'm sure,' continued Jack, 'it must be mighty well worth looking at.'

'You may say that, Jack', said the Merrow, 'and if you meet me here next Monday, just at this time of the day, we will have a little more talk with one another about the matter.'

Jack and the Merrow parted the best friends in the world.

On Monday they met, and Jack was not a

little surprised to see that the Merrow had two cocked hats with him, one under each arm.

'Might I take the liberty to ask, sir,' said Jack, 'why your honour has brought the two hats with you today? You would not, sure, be going to give me one of them to keep for the curiosity of the thing?'

'No, no, Jack,' said he, 'I don't get my hats so easily to part with them that way, but I want you to come down and dine with me, and I brought you the hat to dive with.'

'Lord bless and preserve us!' cried Jack, in amazement, 'would you want me to go down to the bottom of the salt sea ocean? Sure I'd be smothered and choked up with the water, to say nothing of being drowned! And what would poor Biddy do for me, and what would she say?'

'And what matter what she says, you *pinkeen?* Who cares for Biddy's squalling? It's long before your grandfather would have talked in that way. Many's the time he stuck that same hat on his head and dived down boldly after me, and many's the snug bit of dinner and good shellful of brandy he and I have had together below under the water.'

'Is it really, sir, and no joke?' said Jack.

'Why, then, sorrow from me for ever and a day after, if I'll be a bit worse man nor my grandfather was! Here goes — but play me fair now. Here's neck or nothing!' cried Jack.

'That's your grandfather all over,' said the old fellow, 'so come along, then, and do as I do.'

They both left the cave, walked into the sea and then swam a piece until they got to the rock. The Merrow climbed to the top of it and Jack followed him. On the far side it was as straight as the wall of a house, and the sea beneath looked so deep that Jack was almost cowed.

'Now, do you see, Jack,' said the Merrow, 'just put this hat on your head, and mind to keep your eyes wide open. Take hold of my tail, and follow after me and you'll see what you'll see.'

In he dashed and in dashed Jack after him boldly. They went and they went, and Jack thought they'd never stop going. Many a time he wished himself sitting at home by the fireside with Biddy. Yet where was the use of wishing now when he was so many miles as he thought below the waves of the Atlantic? Still he held hard by the Merrow's tail, slippery as it was and, at last, to Jack's great surprise, they got out of the water and he actually found himself on dry land at the bottom of the sea. They landed just in front of a nice house that was slated very neatly with oyster shells and the Merrow, turning about to Jack, welcomed him down.

Jack could hardly speak, what with wonder and what with being out of breath with travelling so fast through the water. He looked about him and could see no living things barring crabs and lobsters of which there were plenty walking leisurely about on the sand. Overhead the sea was like a sky, and the fishes like birds swimming about in it.

'Why don't you speak, man?' said the Merrow. 'I dare say you had no notion that I had such a snug little concern here as this? Are you smothered or choked or drowned, or are you fretting after Biddy, eh?'

'Oh! not myself, indeed,' said Jack, showing his teeth with a good-humoured grin, 'but who in the world would ever have thought of seeing such a thing?'

'Well, come along and let's see what they've got for us to eat?'

Jack really was hungry, and it gave him no small pleasure to see a fine column of smoke rising from the chimney, announcing what was going on within. He followed the Merrow into the house and there he saw a good kitchen, right well provided with everything. There was a noble dresser and plenty of pots and pans, with two young Merrows cooking. His host then led him into the room which was furnished shabbily enough. Not a table or a chair was there in it; nothing but planks and logs of wood to sit on, and eat off. There was, however, a good fire blazing on the hearth — a comfortable sight to Jack.

'Come now, and I'll show you where I keep — you know what,' said the Merrow, with a sly look, and opening a little door, he led Jack into a fine long cellar, well filled with pipes and kegs and hogsheads and barrels.

'What do you say to that, Jack Dogherty? — Eh! — maybe a body can't live snug under the water?'

'Never the doubt of that,' said Jack, with a convincing smack of his under lip, to show that he really thought what he said.

They went back to the room and found dinner ready. There was no tablecloth, to be sure — but what matter? It was not always Jack had one at home. The dinner would have been no discredit to the first house of the county on a fast day. The choicest of fish, and no wonder, was there, turbots, soles, lobsters, oysters and twenty other kinds were on the planks at once, and plenty of the best foreign spirits. The wines, the old fellow said, were too cold for his stomach.

Jack ate and drank till he could eat no more. Then, taking up a shell of brandy, 'Here's to your honour's good health, sir,' said he, 'though, begging your pardon, it's mighty odd that as long as we've been acquainted I don't know your name yet.'

'That's true, Jack,' he replied. 'I never thought of it before, but better late than never. My name's Coomara.'

'And a mighty decent name it is,' cried Jack, taking another shellful. 'Here's to your good health, Coomara, and may you live these fifty years to come!'

'Fifty years!' repeated Coomara, 'I'm obliged to you, indeed! If you had said five hundred it would have been something worth the wishing.'

'By the laws, sir,' cried Jack, 'you live to a powerful age here under the water! You knew my grandfather and he's dead and gone better than these sixty years. I'm sure it must be a mighty healthy place to live in.'

'No doubt of it, but come, Jack, keep the liquor stirring.' Shell after shell did they empty, and to Jack's exceeding surprise, he found the drink never got into his head, owing, I suppose, to the sea being over them, which kept their noddles cool.

Old Coomara got exceedingly comfortable and sang several songs; but Jack, if his life had depended on it, never could remember more than

> Rum fum boodle boo,
>   Ripple dipple nitty dob;
> Dumdoo doodle coo,
>   Raffle taffle chittibob!

It was the chorus to one of them, and to tell the truth, nobody that I know has ever been able to pick any particular meaning out of it; but that, to be sure, is the case with many a song nowadays.

At length he said to Jack, 'Now, my dear boy, if you follow me, I'll show you my curiosities!' He opened a little door and led Jack into a large room where Jack saw a great many odds and ends that Coomara had picked up at one time or another. What chiefly took his attention, however, were things like lobster-pots ranged on the ground along the wall.

'Well, Jack, how do you like my curiosities?' said old Coo.

'Upon my sowkins, sir,' said Jack, 'they're mighty well worth the looking at, but might I make so bold as to ask what these things like lobster-pots are?'

'Oh! the Soul Cages, is it?'

'The what? sir!'

'These things here that I keep the souls in.'

'Arrah! what souls, sir?' said Jack, in amazement. 'Sure the fish have got no souls in them?'

'Oh! no,' replied Coo, quite coolly, 'that they have not; but these are the souls of drowned sailors.'

'The Lord preserve us from all harm!' muttered Jack, 'how in the world did you get them?'

'Easily enough. When I see a good storm coming on, I've only to set a couple of dozen of these, and then, when the sailors are drowned and the souls get out of them under the water, the poor things are almost perished to death not being used to the cold, so they make into my pots for shelter, and then I have them snug

and fetch them home and keep them here dry and warm; and is it not well for the poor souls to get into such good quarters?'

Jack was so thunderstruck he did not know what to say, so he said nothing. They went back into the dining room, and had a little more brandy, which was excellent, and then, as Jack knew that it must be getting late, and as Biddy might be uneasy, he stood up and said he thought it was time for him to be on the road.

'Just as you like, Jack,' said Coo, 'but take a *deoc an dorais* before you go; you've a cold journey before you.'

Jack knew better manners than to refuse the parting glass. 'I wonder,' said he, 'will I be able to make out my way home?'

'What should ail you,' said Coo, 'when I'll show you the way?'

Out they went before the house, and Coomara took one of the cocked hats and put it upon Jack's head the wrong way, and then lifted him up on his shoulder that he might launch him up into the water.

'Now,' says he, giving him a heave, 'you'll come up just in the same spot you came down in, and, Jack, mind and throw me back the hat.'

He canted Jack off his shoulder and up he

shot like a bubble — whirr, whirr, whiz — away he went up through the water till he came to the very rock he had jumped off, where he found a landing-place, and then in he threw the hat which sank like a stone.

The sun was just going down in the beautiful sky of a calm summer's evening. Feascor was seen dimly twinkling in the cloudless heaven, a solitary star, and the waves of the Atlantic flashed in a golden flood of light. So Jack, seeing it was late, set off home but when he got there not a word did he say to Biddy of where he had spent his day.

The state of the poor souls cooped up in the lobster-pots gave Jack a great deal of trouble, and how to release them cost him a great deal of thought. He at first had a mind to speak to the priest about the matter. But what could the priest do, and what did Coo care for the priest? Besides, Coo was a good sort of an old fellow and did not think he was doing any harm. Jack had a regard for him too, and it also might not be much to his own credit if it were known that he used to go dine with Merrows. On the whole he thought his best plan would be to ask Coo to dinner and to make him drunk, if he was able, and then to take the hat and go down and turn up the pots. It was first of all necessary, how-ever, to get Biddy out of the way, for Jack was prudent enough, as she was a woman, to wish to keep the thing secret from her.

Accordingly, Jack grew mighty pious all of a sudden and said to Biddy that he thought it would be for the good of both of their souls if she was to go and make her rounds at Saint John's Well near Ennis. Biddy thought so too, and so she set off one fine morning at dawn, giving Jack a strict charge to have an eye to the place.

The coast being clear, away went Jack to the rock to give the appointed signal to Coomara, which was throwing a big stone into the water. Jack threw it and up sprang Coo!

'Good morrow, Jack,' said he. 'What do you want with me?'

'Just nothing at all to speak about, sir,' replied Jack, 'only to come and take a bit of dinner with me, if I might make so free as to ask you, and sure I'm now after doing so.'

'It's quite agreeable, Jack, I assure you — at what time?'

'Any time that's most convenient to you, sir — say one o'clock, that you may go home, if you wish, with the daylight.'

'I'll be with you,' said Coo, 'never fear me.'

Jack went home and dressed a noble fish dinner, and got out plenty of his best foreign spirits, enough for that matter to make twenty men drunk. Just to the minute Coo came with his cocked hat under his arm. Dinner was ready — they sat down, and ate and drank away manfully. Jack, thinking of the poor souls below in the pots, plied old Coo well with brandy, and encouraged him to sing, hoping to put him under the table, but poor Jack forgot that he had not the sea over his own head to keep it cool. The brandy got into it and did his business for him, and Coo reeled off home leaving his entertainer as dumb as a haddock on a Good Friday.

Jack never woke till the next morning and then he was in a sad way. ''Tis to no use for me thinking to make that old Rapparee drunk,' said Jack, 'and how in this world can I help the poor souls out of the lobster-pots?' Having thought nearly the whole day, an idea struck him. 'I have it,' says he, slapping his knee. 'I'll be sworn that Coo never saw a drop of poteen, as old as he is, and that's the thing to settle him! Oh! then, is not it well that Biddy will not be home these two days yet — I can have another twist at him.'

Jack asked Coo again, and Coo laughed at him for having no better head, telling him he'd never come up to his grandfather.

'Well, but try me again,' said Jack, 'and I'll be bail to drink you drunk and sober, and drunk again.'

'Anything in my power,' said Coo, 'to oblige you.'

At this dinner Jack took care to have his own liquor well watered, and to give the strongest brandy he had to Coo. At last, says he, 'Pray, sir, did you ever drink any poteen — any real mountain dew?'

'No,' says Coo. 'What's that and where does it come from?'

'Oh, that's a secret,' said Jack, 'but it's the right stuff — never believe me again, if 'tis not fifty times as good as brandy or rum either. Biddy's brother just sent me a present of a little drop in exchange for some brandy, and as you're an old friend of the family, I kept it to treat you with.'

'Well, let's see what sort of thing it is,' said Coomara.

The poteen was the right sort. It was first rate and had the real smack upon it. Coo was delighted. He drank and he sang 'Rum bum boodle boo' over and over again, and he laughed and he danced till he fell on the floor fast asleep. Then Jack, who had taken good care to keep himself sober, snapped up the cocked hat, ran off to the rock, leaped in and soon arrived at Coo's habitation.

All was as still as a churchyard at midnight — not a Merrow old or young was there. In he went and turned up the pots, but nothing did he see, only he heard a sort of a little whistle or chirp as he raised each of them. At this he was surprised till he recollected what the priest had often said, that nobody living could see the soul no more than they could see the wind or the air! Having now done all that he could do for them he set the pots as they were before, and sent a blessing after the poor souls to speed them on their journey wherever they were going. Jack now began to think of returning; he put the hat on as was right, the wrong way, but when he got out, he found the water so high over his head that he had no hopes of ever getting up into it now that he had not old Coomara to give him a lift. He walked about looking for a ladder but not one could he find and not a rock was there in sight. At last he saw a spot where the sea hung rather lower than anywhere else, so he resolved to try there. Just as he came to it a big cod happened to put down his tail. Jack made a jump and caught hold of it, and the cod, all in amazement, gave a bounce and pulled Jack up. The minute the hat touched the water, pop away Jack was whisked, and up he shot like a cork, dragging the poor cod that he forgot to let go, up with him, tail foremost. He got to the rock in no time and without a moment's delay hurried home, rejoicing in the good deed he had done. But, meanwhile, there was fine work at home, for our friend Jack had hardly left the house on his soul-freeing expedition when back came Biddy from her soul-saving one to the well. When she entered the house and saw the things lying topsy-turvey on the table before her —

'Here's a pretty job!' said she — 'that blackguard of mine — what ill-luck I had ever to marry him! He has picked up some vagabond or other, while I was praying for the good of his soul, and they've been drinking all the poteen that my own brother gave him, and all the spirits, to be sure, that he was to have sold to his honour.'

Then hearing an outlandish kind of grunt,

she looked down and saw Coomara lying under the table.

'The blessed Virgin help me,' she shouted, 'if he has not made a real beast of himself! Well, well, I've often heard of a man making a beast of himself with drink! Jack, honey, what will I do with you, or what will I do without you? How can any decent woman ever think of living with a beast?'

With such like lamentations Biddy rushed out of the house, and was going, she knew not where, when she heard the well-known voice of Jack singing a merry tune. Glad enough was Biddy to find him safe and sound, and not turned into a thing that was like neither fish nor flesh. Jack was obliged to tell her all, and Biddy, though she had half a mind to be angry with him for not telling her before, owned that he had done a great service to the poor souls. Back they both went most lovingly to the house and Jack wakened up Coomara, and seeing the old fellow to be rather dull, he bid him not be cast down, and said it all came of his not being used to the poteen and recommended him, by way of cure, to swallow a hair of the dog that bit him. Coo, however, seemed to think he had had quite enough. He got up, quite out of sorts, and without having the manners to say one word in the way of civility, he sneaked off to cool himself by a jaunt through the salt water.

Coomara never missed the souls. He and Jack continued to be the best friends in the world, and no one, perhaps, ever equalled Jack at freeing souls from purgatory, for he contrived fifty excuses for getting into the house below the sea, unknown to the old fellow, and then turning up the pots and letting out the souls. It vexed him, to be sure, that he could never see them, but as he knew the thing to be impossible he was obliged to be satisfied.

Their intercourse continued for several years. However, one morning, on Jack's throwing in a stone as usual, he got no answer. He flung another and another; still there was no reply. He went away and returned the following morning, but it was to no purpose. As he was without the hat, he could not go down to see what had become of old Coo, but his belief was that the old man, or the old fish, or whatever he was, had either died or had moved away from that part of the country.

# 4

# The Legend of Knocksheogowna

In Tipperary is one of the most singularly shaped hills in the world. It has got a peak at the top like a conical nightcap thrown carelessly over your head as you awake in the morning. On the very point is built a sort of lodge, where in the summer the lady who built it and her friends used to go on parties of pleasure; but that was long after the days of the fairies, and it is, I believe, now deserted.

But before the lodge was built or acre sown, there was close to the head of this hill a large pasturage, where a herdsman spent his days and nights among the herd. The spot had been an old fairy ground, and the good people were angry that the scene of their light and airy gambols should be trampled by the rude hoofs of bulls and cows. The lowing of the cattle sounded sad in their ears, and the chief of the fairies of the hill determined in person to drive away the new comers, and the way she thought of was this. When the harvest nights came on, and the moon shone bright and brilliant over the hill, and the cattle were lying down hushed and quiet, and the herdsman, wrapped in his mantle, was dreaming with his heart gladdened by the glorious company of the stars twinkling above him, she would come and dance before him — now in one shape — now in another — but all ugly and frightful to behold. One time she would be a great horse with the wings of an eagle and a tail like a dragon, hissing loud and spitting fire. Then in a moment she would change into a little man, lame of a leg, with a bull's head, and a lambent flame playing around it. Then into a great ape with duck's feet and a turkey-cock's tail. But I should be all day about it were I to tell you all the shapes she took. And then she would roar, or neigh, or hiss, or bellow, or howl, or hoot, as never yet was roaring, neighing, hissing, bellowing, howling, or hooting heard in this world before or since. The poor herdsman would cover his face, and call on all the saints for help, but it was no use. With one puff of her breath she would blow away the

fold of his great coat, let him hold it ever so tightly over his eyes, and not a saint in heaven paid him the slightest attention. And to make matters worse, he never could stir; no, nor even shut his eyes, but there was obliged to stay, held by what power he knew not, gazing at these terrible sights until the hair of his head would lift his hat half a foot over his crown, and his teeth would be ready to fall out from chattering. But the cattle would scamper about mad, as if they were bitten by the fly; and this would last until the sun rose over the hill.

The poor cattle were pining away from want of rest, and food did them no good; besides, they met with accidents without end. Never a night passed that some of them did not fall into a pit and get maimed, or maybe killed. Some would tumble into a river and be drowned. In a word, there seemed never to be an end to the accidents. But what made the matter worse, a herdsman could not be got to tend the cattle by night. One visit from the fairy drove the stoutest-hearted almost mad. The owner of the ground did not know what to do. He offered double, treble, quadruple wages, but not a man could be found for the sake of money to go through the horror of facing the fairy. She rejoiced at the successful issue of her project and continued her pranks. The herd gradually thinning, and no man daring to remain on the ground, the fairies came back in numbers, and gambolled as merrily as before, quaffing dew-drops from acorns, and spreading their feast on the head of capacious mushrooms.

What was to be done, the puzzled farmer wondered in vain. He found that his substance was daily diminishing, his people terrified, and his rent-day coming round. It is no wonder that he looked gloomy, and walked mournfully down the road.

Now in that part of the world dwelt a man of the name of Larry Hoolahan, who played on the pipes better than any other player within fifteen parishes. A roving, dashing blade was Larry, and feared nothing. Give him plenty of liquor and he would defy the devil. He would face a mad bull, or fight single-handed against a fair. In one of his gloomy walks the farmer met him, and on Larry's asking the cause of his down looks, he told him all his misfortunes. 'If that is all ails you,' said Larry, 'make your mind easy. Were there as many fairies on Knock-sheogowna as there are potato blossoms in Eliogurty (a barony in Co. Tipperary remark-

able for its fertility), I would face them. It would be a queer thing, indeed, if I, who never was afraid of a proper man, should turn my back upon a brat of a fairy not the bigness of one's thumb.'

'Larry,' said the farmer, 'do not talk so bold, for you know not who is hearing you; but, if you make your words good, and watch my herds for a week on the top of the mountain, your hand shall be free of my dish till the sun has burnt itself down to the bigness of a farthing rushlight.'

The bargain was struck and Larry went to the hilltop when the moon began to peep over the brow. He had been regaled at the farmer's house and was bold with the extract of barley-corn. So he took his seat on a big stone under a hollow of the hill with his back to the wind, and pulled out his pipes. He had not played long when the voice of the fairies was heard upon the blast, like a low stream of music. Presently they burst out into a loud laugh and Larry could plainly hear one say, 'What! another man upon the fairies' ring? Go to him, queen, and make him repent his rashness,' and they flew away. Larry felt them pass by his face as they flew like a swarm of midges, and looking up hastily, he saw between the moon and himself a great black cat standing on the very tip of its claws, with its back up and mewing with a voice of a water-mill. Presently it swelled up towards the sky and, turning round on its left hind leg, whirled till it fell to the ground, from which it started in the shape of a salmon with a cravat round its neck and a pair of new top-boots.

'Go on, jewel,' said Larry, 'if you dance, I'll pipe,' and he struck up. So she turned into this and that and the other, but still Larry played on, as he well knew how. At last she lost patience, as ladies will do when you do not mind their scolding, and changed herself into a calf, milk-white as the cream of Cork, and with eyes as mild as those of the girl I love. She came up gentle and fawning in hopes to throw him off his guard by quietness, and then to work him some wrong. But Larry was not so deceived, for when she came up, he, dropping his pipes, leaped upon her back.

Now from the top of Knocksheogowna, as you look westward to the broad Atlantic, you will see the Shannon, queen of rivers, 'spreading like a sea', and running on in gentle course to mingle with the ocean through the fair city of Limerick. On this night it shone under the moon and looked beautiful from the distant hill. Fifty boats were gliding up and down on the sweet current and the song of the fishermen rose gaily from the shore. Larry, as I said before, leaped upon the back of the fairy and she, rejoicing at the opportunity, sprang from the hilltop and bounded clear, at one jump, over the Shannon, flowing as it was just ten miles from the mountain's base. It was done in a second, and when she alighted on the distant bank, kicking up her heels, she flung Larry on the soft turf. No sooner was he thus planted than he looked her straight in the face and, scratching his head, cried out, 'By my word, well done! That was not a bad leap for a calf!'

She looked at him for a moment and then assumed her own shape. 'Laurence,' she said, 'you are a bold fellow. Will you come back the way you went?'

'And that's what I will,' said he, 'if you let me.' So changing to a calf again, Larry again got on her back, and at another bound they were again upon the top of Knocksheogowna. The fairy once more resuming her figure, addressed him, 'You have shown so much courage, Laurence,' said she, 'that while you keep herds on this hill you shall never be molested by me or mine. When day dawns go down to the farmer and tell him this, and if anything I can do may be of service to you, ask and you shall have it.' She vanished accordingly and kept her word in never visiting the hill during Larry's life, but he never troubled her with requests. He piped and drank at the farmer's expense, and roosted in his chimney corner, occasionally casting an eye to the flock. He died at last and is buried in a green valley of pleasant Tipperary. But whether the fairies retured to the hill of Knocksheogowna after his death is more than I can say.

# 5

# Fior Usga

A little way beyond the Gallows Green of
Cork, and just outside the town, there is a great
lough of water where people in the winter go
and skate for the sake of diversion. But the
sport above the water is nothing to what is
under it, for at the very bottom of this lough
there are buildings and gardens far more beautiful than any now to be seen, and how they came
there was in this manner.

Long before Saxon foot pressed Irish
ground, there was a great king called Corc,
whose palace stood where the lough now is, in a
round green valley that was just a mile wide. In
the middle of the courtyard was a spring of fair
water, so pure and so clear that it was the
wonder of all the world. The king rejoiced at
having so great a curiosity within his palace, but
as people came in crowds from far and near to
draw the precious water of this spring he was
sorely afraid that in time it might become dry.

So he caused a high wall to be built up round it
and would allow nobody to have the water,
which was a very great loss to the poor people
living about the palace. Whenever he wanted
any for himself he would send his daughter to
get it, not liking to trust his servants with the
key of the well-door, fearing they might give
some away.

One night the king gave a grand party, and
there were many great princes present and lords
and nobles without end. And there were
wonderful doings throughout the palace. There
were bonfires, whose blaze reached up to the
very sky; and there was dancing to such sweet
music that it ought to have woken up the dead
out of the graves; and feasting in the greatest of
plenty for all who came. Nor was anyone
turned away from the palace gates — but
'you're welcome — you're welcome, heartily,'
was the porter's salute for all.

Now it happened at this grand party there
was one young prince above all the rest mighty
comely to behold, and as tall and as straight as
ever an eye would wish to look on. Right
merrily did he dance that night with the old
king's daughter, wheeling here and wheeling
there, as light as a feather, and footing it away

to the admiration of everyone. The musicians played the better for seeing their dancing and they danced as if their lives depended upon it. After all this dancing came the supper, and the young prince was seated at table by the side of his beautiful partner who smiled upon him as often as he spoke to her; and that was by no means so often as he wished, for he had constantly to turn to the company and thank them for the many compliments passed upon his fair partner and himself.

In the midst of this banquet one of the great lords said to King Corc, 'May it please your majesty, here is every thing in abundance that the heart can wish for both to eat and drink except water.'

'Water!' said the king, mightily pleased at someone calling for that of which purposely there was a want: 'Water shall you have, my lord, speedily and that of such a delicious kind that I challenge all the world to equal it. Daughter,' he said, 'go fetch some in the golden vessel which I caused to be made for the purpose.'

The king's daughter, who was called Fior Usga (which signifies in English 'spring water'), did not much like to be told to perform so menial a service before so many people, and though she did not venture to refuse the commands of her father yet hesitated to obey him and looked down upon the ground. The king, who loved his daughter very much, seeing this, was sorry for what he had desired her to do, but having said the word, he was never known to recall it. He therefore thought of a way to make his daughter go speedily and fetch the water, and it was by proposing that the young prince her partner should go along with her. Accordingly, with a loud voice, he said, 'Daughter, I wonder not at your fearing to go alone so late at night, but I doubt not the young prince at your side will go with you.' The prince was not displeased at hearing this, and taking the golden vessel in one hand, with the other he led the king's daughter out of the hall so gracefully that all present gazed after them with delight.

When they came to the spring of water in the courtyard of the palace, Fior Usga unlocked the door with the greatest care and stooping down with the golden vessel to take some of the water out of the well, found the vessel so heavy that she lost her balance and fell in. The young prince tried in vain to save her, for the water rose and rose so fast that the entire courtyard was speedily covered with it, and he hastened back almost in a state of distraction to the king.

The door of the well being left open, the water which had been so long confined, rejoiced at obtaining its liberty, rushed forth incessantly every moment rising higher and was in the hall of the entertainment sooner than the young prince himself, so that when he attempted to speak to the king he was up to his neck in water. At length the water rose to such a height that it filled the entire green valley in which the king's palace stood, and so the present lough of Cork was formed.

Yet the king and his guests were not drowned as would now happen if such an awful inundation were to take place; neither was his daughter, the fair Usga, who returned to the banquet hall the very next night after this dreadful event. And every night since the same party and dancing goes on in the palace in the bottom of the lough, and will last until someone has the luck to bring up out of it the golden vessel which was the cause of all this mischief.

Nobody can doubt that it was a judgment upon the king for his shutting up the well in the courtyard from the poor people, and if there are

any who do not credit my story, they may go and see the lough of Cork, for there it is to be seen to this day. The road to Kinsale passes at one side of it, and when its waters are low and clear the tops of the towers and stately buildings may be plainly viewed in the bottom by those who have good eyesight, without the help of spectacles.

# 6

# Rent-Day

'Oh ullagone, ullagone! this is a wide world, but what will we do in it, or where will we go?' muttered Bill Doody, as he sat on a rock by the Lake of Killarney. 'What will we do? To-morrow's rent-day, and Tim the Driver swears if we don't pay up our rent, he'll take every-thing we have, and then, sure enough, Judy and myself, and the poor little children will be turned out to starve on the high road, for the never a halfpenny of rent have I! — Oh hone, that ever I should live to see this day!'

Thus did Bill Doody bemoan his hard fate, pouring his sorrows to the reckless waves of the most beautiful of lakes, which seemed to mock his misery as they rejoiced beneath the cloud-less sky of a May morning. That lake, glittering in sunshine, sprinkled with fairy isles of rock and verdure and bounded by giant hills of ever-varying hues, might with its magic beauty charm all sadness but despair, for alas,

How ill the scene that offers rest
And heart that cannot rest agree!

Yet Bill Doody was not so desolate as he supposed. There was one listening to him he little thought of, and help was at hand from a quarter he could not have expected.

'What's the matter with you, my poor man?' said a tall portly-looking gentleman, at the same time stepping out of a furze-brake. Now Bill was seated on a rock that commanded a view of a large field. Nothing in the field could be concealed from him except this furze-brake which grew in a hollow near the margin of the lake. He was, therefore, not a little surprised at the gentleman's sudden appearance, and began to question whether the personage before him belonged to this world or not. He, however, soon mustered sufficient courage to tell him how his crops had failed, how some bad member had charmed away his butter, and how Tim the Driver threatened to turn him out of the farm if he didn't pay up every penny of the rent by twelve o'clock next day.

'A sad story, indeed,' said the stranger, 'but surely, if you represented the case to your landlord's agent, he won't have the heart to turn you out.'

'Heart, your honour! Where would an agent get a heart!' exclaimed Bill. 'I see your honour does not know him. Besides, he has an eye on the farm this long time for a fosterer of his own, so I expect no mercy at all at all, only to be turned out.'

'Take this, my poor fellow, take this,' said the stranger, pouring a purse full of gold into Bill's old hat, which in his grief he had flung on the ground. 'Pay the fellow your rent, but I'll take care it shall do him no good. I remember the time when things went otherwise in this country, when I would have hung up such a fellow in the twinkling of an eye!'

These words were lost upon Bill who was insensible to everything but the sight of the gold, and before he could unfix his gaze and lift up his head to pour out his hundred thousand blessings the stranger was gone. The bewildered peasant looked around in search of his benefactor, and at last he thought he saw him riding on a white horse a long way off on the lake.

'O'Donoghue, O'Donoghue!' shouted Bill, 'the good, the blessed O'Donoghue!' and he ran capering like a madman to show Judy the

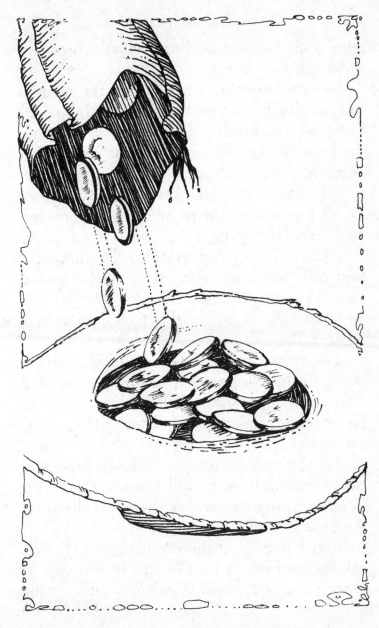

gold, and to rejoice her heart with the prospect of wealth and happiness.

The next day Bill proceeded to the agent's, not sneakingly with his hat in his hand, his eyes fixed on the ground and his knees bending under him, but bold and upright like a man conscious of his independence.

'Why don't you take off your hat, fellow? Don't you know you are speaking to a magistrate?' said the agent.

'I know I'm not speaking to the king, sir,' said Bill, 'and I never takes off my hat but to them I can respect and love. The Eye that sees all knows I've no right either to respect or love an agent!'

'You scoundrel!' retorted the man in office, biting his lips with rage at such an unusual and unexpected opposition, 'I'll teach you how to be insolent again — I have the power, remember.'

'To the cost of the country, I know you have,' said Bill, who still remained with his head as firmly covered as if he was the Lord Kingsale himself.

'But, come,' said the magistrate, 'have you got the money for me? — this is rent-day. If there's one penny of it wanting, or the running gale that's due, prepare to turn out before night, for you shall not remain another hour in possession.'

'There is your rent,' said Bill, with an unmoved expression of tone and countenance. 'You'd better count it and give me a receipt in full for the running gale and all.'

The agent gave a look of amazement at the gold, for it was gold — real guineas, and not bits of dirty ragged small notes that are only fit to light one's pipe with. However willing the agent may have been to ruin, as he thought, the unfortunate tenant, he took up the gold and handed the receipt to Bill who strutted off with it as proud as a cat of her whiskers.

The agent going to his desk shortly afterwards was confounded at beholding a heap of gingerbeard cakes instead of the money he had deposited there. He raved and swore but all to no purpose. The gold had become gingerbread cakes, just marked like the guineas with the king's head, and Bill had the receipt in his pocket, so he saw there was no use in saying anything about the affair as he would only get laughed at for his pains.

From that hour Bill Doody grew rich, all his undertakings prospered, and he often blesses the day that he met with O'Donoghue, the great prince that lives down under the Lake of Killarney.

# 7

# The Enchanted Lake

In the west of Ireland there was a lake, and no doubt it is there still, in which many young men were at various times drowned. What made the circumstance remarkable was that the bodies of the drowned persons were never found. People naturally wondered at this; and at length the lake came to have a bad repute. Many dreadful stories were told about that lake: some would affirm that on a dark night its waters appeared like fire — others would speak of horrid forms which were seen to glide over it; and everyone agreed that a strange sulphureous smell issued from out of it.

There lived, not far from this lake, a young farmer, named Roderick Keating, who was about to be married to one of the prettiest girls in that part of the country. On his return from Limerick, where he had been to purchase the wedding-ring, he met two or three of his acquaintances, who were standing on the bank, and they began to joke him about Peggy Honan. One said that young Delaney, his rival, had in his absence contrived to win the affections of his mistress; but Roderick's confidence in his intended bride was too great to be disturbed at this tale, and putting his hand in his pocket, he produced and held up with a significant look the wedding-ring. As he was turning it between his forefinger and thumb, in token of triumph, somehow or other the ring fell from his hand, and rolled into the lake. Roderick looked after it with the greatest sorrow; it was not so much for its value, though it had cost him half a guinea, as for the ill-luck of the thing; and the water was so deep that there was little chance of recovering it. His companions laughed at him, and he tried in vain to tempt any of them by the offer of a handsome reward to dive in after the ring; they were all as little inclined to venture as Roderick Keating himself; for the tales which they had heard when children were strongly impressed on their memories, and a superstitious dread filled the minds of each.

'Must I then go back to Limerick to buy another ring?' exclaimed the young farmer. 'Will not ten times what the ring cost tempt any one of you to venture after it?'

There was within hearing a man who was considered to be a poor, crazy, half-witted fellow, but he was as harmless as a child, and used to go wandering up and down through the country from one place to another. When he heard of so great a reward, Paddeen, for that was his name, spoke out, and said that if Roderick Keating would give him encouragement equal to what he had offered to others, he was ready to venture after the ring into the lake; and Paddeen, all the while he spoke, looked as covetous after the sport as the money.

'I'll take you at your word,' said Keating. So Paddeen pulled off his coat, and without a single syllable more, down he plunged, head foremost, into the lake: what depth he went to, no one can tell exactly; but he was going, going, going down through the water until the water parted from him, and he came upon the dry land: the sky, and the light, and everything, was there just as it is here; and he saw fine pleasure-grounds, with an elegant avenue through them, and a grand house, with a power of steps going up to the door. When he had recovered from his wonder at finding the land so dry and comfortable under the water, he looked about him, and what should he see but all the young men that were drowned working away in the pleasure-grounds as if nothing had ever happened to them. Some of them were mowing down the grass, and more were settling out the gravel walks, and doing all manner of nice work, as neat and as clever as if they had never been drowned; and they were singing away with high glee:

> She is fair as Cappoquin:
> Have you courage her to win?
> And her wealth it far but shines
> Cullen's bog and Silvermines.
> She exceeds all heart can wish;
> Not brawling like the Foherish,
> But as the brightly-flowing Lee,
> Graceful, mild, and pure is she!

Well, Paddeen could not but look at the young men, for he knew some of them before they were lost in the lake; but he said nothing, though he thought a great deal more for all that, like an oyster: no, not the wind of a word passed his lips; so on he went towards the big house, bold enough, as if he had seen nothing to speak of; yet all the time wishing to know who the young woman could be that the young men were singing the song about.

When he had nearly reached the door of the great house, out walks a powerful fat woman from the kitchen, moving along like a beer-barrel on two legs, with teeth as big as horse's teeth, and up she made towards him.

'Good morrow, Paddeen,' said she.

'Good morrow, Ma'am,' said he.

'What brought you here?' said she.

''Tis after Rory Keating's gold ring,' said he, 'I'm come.'

'Here it is for you,' said Paddeen's fat friend, with a smile on her face that moved like boiling stirabout (gruel).

'Thank you, Ma'am,' replied Paddeen, taking it from her. 'I need not say the Lord increase you, for you're fat enough already. Will you tell me, if you please, am I to go back the same way I came?'

'Then you did not come to marry me?' cried the corpulent woman, in a desperate fury.

'Just wait till I come back again, my darling,' said Paddeen. 'I'm to be paid for my message, and I must return with the answer, or else they'll wonder what has become of me.'

'Never mind the money,' said the fat woman. 'If you marry me you shall live for ever and a day in that house, and want for nothing.'

Paddeen saw clearly that, having got possession of the ring, the fat woman had no power to detain him; so without minding anything she said, he kept moving and moving down the avenue, quite quietly, and looking about him; for, to tell the truth, he had no particular inclination to marry a fat fairy. When he came to the gate, without ever   saying goodbye, out he bolted, and he found the water coming all about him again. Up he plunged through it, and wonder enough there was, when Paddeen was seen swimming away at the opposite side of the lake; but he soon reached the shore, and told Roderick Keating and the other boys that were standing there looking out for him all that had happened. Roderick paid him the five guineas for the ring on the spot; and Paddeen thought himself so rich with such a sum of money in his pocket, that he did not go back to marry the fat lady with the fine house at the bottom of the lake, knowing she had plenty of young men to choose a husband from if she pleased to be married.

# *MORE MERCIER BESTSELLERS*

## TALES OF IRISH ENCHANTMENT
## Patricia Lynch

Patricia Lynch brings to this selection of classical Irish folktales for young people all the imagination and warmth for which she is renowned.

There are seven stories here: Midir and Etain, The Quest of the Sons of Turenn, The Swan Children, Deirdre and the Sons of Usna, Labra the Mariner, Cuchulain – The Champion of Ireland and The Voyage of Maeldun.

They lose none of their original appeal in the retelling and are as delightful today as when they were first told.

The stories are greatly enhanced by the immediacy and strength of Frances Boland's imaginative drawings.

## ENCHANTED IRISH TALES
## Patricia Lynch

*Enchanted Irish Tales* tells of ancient heroes and heroines, fantastic deeds of bravery, magical kingdoms, weird and wonderful animals... This new illustrated edition of classical folktales, retold by Patricia Lynch with all the imagination and warmth for which she is renowned, rekindles the age-old legends of Ireland, as exciting today as they were when first told. The collection includes:

- Conary Mór and the Three Red Riders
- The Long Life of Tuan Mac Carrell
- Finn Mac Cool and Fianna
- Oisin and The Land of Youth
- The Kingdom of The Dwarfs
- The Dragon Ring of Connla
- Mac Datho's Boar
- Ethne

# IRISH FAIRY TALES
## Michael Scott

'He found he was staring directly at a leprechaun. The small man was sitting on a little mound of earth beneath the shade of a weeping willow tree... The young man could feel his heart beginning to pound. He had seen leprechauns a few times before but only from a distance. They were very hard to catch, but if you managed at all to get hold of one...'

Michael Scott's exciting stories capture all the magic and mystery of Irish folklore. This collection of twelve fairy tales, beautifully and unusually illustrated, include:

The arrival of the Tuatha de Danann in Erin

| | |
|---|---|
| The fairy horses | The King's secret |
| The crow goddess | The fairies' revenge |
| The wise woman's payment | The shoemaker and himself |
| The floating island | The sunken town |

# IRISH ANIMAL TALES
## Michael Scott

'Have you ever noticed how cats and dogs sometimes sit up and look at something that is not there? Have you ever seen a dog barking at nothing? And have you ever wondered why? Perhaps it is because the animals can see the fairy folk coming and going all the time, while humans can only see the little People at certain times...'

This illustrated collection of Michael Scott's strange stories reveal a wealth of magical creatures that inhabit Ireland's enchanted animal kingdom. The tales tell of the king of the cats, the magical cows, the fox and the hedgehog, the dog and the leprechaun, March, April and the Brindled Cow, the cricket's tale... A collection to entrance readers, both young and old.

# THE CHILDREN'S BOOK OF IRISH FAIRY TALES
## PATRICIA DUNN

The five exciting stories in this book tell of the mythical, enchanted origins of Irish landmarks when the countryside was peopled with good fairies, wicked witches, gallant heroes and beautiful princesses.

Did you know that there are bright, shimmering lakes in Killarney concealing submerged castles, mountain peaks in Wexford created by magic, a dancing bush in Cork bearing lifesaving berries, the remains of a witch in a Kerry field and deer with silver and golden horns around Lough Gartan and Donegal?

These stories tell of extraordinary happenings long, long ago and show that evidence of these exciting events can still be seen today if you only take the time to look carefully.

## STRANGE IRISH TALES FOR CHILDREN
## Edmund Lenihan

*Strange Irish Tales for Children* is a collection of four hilarious stories, by seanchaí Edmund Lenihan, which will entertain and amuse children of all ages.

The stories tell of the adventures of the Fianna and about Fionn MacCumhail's journey to Norway in search of a blackbird. There is a fascinating tale about 'The Strange Case of Seán na Súl' whose job was to kidnap people to take them away to a magic island. 'Taoscán MacLiath and the Magic Bees' is a story about the exploits of this very famous druid and about how he packed his spell-books and took himself off to the conference held by the druids of the Seven Lands.

## STORIES OF OLD IRELAND FOR CHILDREN
## Edmund Lenihan

Long ago in Ireland there were men who used to travel to the four ends of the earth and few travelled farther than Fionn and the men of the Fianna during their many exciting adventures. In 'Stories of Old Ireland for Children' we read about 'Fionn Mac Cumhail and Feathers of China', 'King Cormac's Fighting Academy', and 'Fionn and the Mermaids'.

## THE CHILDREN'S BOOK OF IRISH FOLKTALES
## Kevin Danaher

These tales are filled with the mystery and adventure of a land of lonely country roads and isolated farms, humble cottages and lordly castles, rolling fields and tractless bogs. They tell of giants and ghosts, of queer happenings and wondrous deeds, of fairies and witches and of fools and kings.

## IRISH LEGENDS FOR CHILDREN
## Lady Gregory

Traditional legends told for children, including 'The Fate of the Children of Lir', 'The Coming of Finn', 'Finn's Household', and 'The Best Men of the Fianna'.

## SCARY POEMS FOR ROTTEN KIDS
### sean o huigin

The poems focus on what the author says are the most monstrous episodes in the life of any ordinary child. With characteristic humour o huigin describes *Scary Poems* as 'the perfect book to give to kids you hate'. More than 130,000 copies of this international bestseller in print.


## MONSTERS, HE MUMBLED
### sean o huigin

In *Monsters, He Mumbled*, a collection of verse, o huigin presents a host of bizarre situations from monsters oozing out of toothpaste to creatures nibbling off toes.